STITCH'S STORY
ADVENTURES OF A RESCUE DOG

WRITTEN & PHOTOGRAPHED
BY LAURA FOGARTY

SocialMotion
PUBLISHING

Published by Social Motion Publishing,
the first and only publisher in the
United States dedicated to social-impact books:
SocialMotionPublishing.com

ISBN: 978-0-9704379-3-8

Produced in the United States of America

Stitch's Story *is dedicated to my Mom,*
who introduced me to the unwavering loyalty
and unconditional love of dogs.

Margery Fogarty
December 2, 1941–July 23, 2017

"You can judge a person's true character
by the way they treat their fellow animals."
Paul McCartney

Hi, my name is Stitch, and I am a pretty special dog. I am not just a very loved pet, but I also have an important job as a therapy dog.

It wasn't always this way. I used to have no home and no family. One day I crossed paths with some very caring people who believed in me and knew I was created to do great things.

This is my story.

"You are the hero of your own story."
Joseph Campbell

German short-haired pointer

Photo by Milian vom Nonnenhaus

    A lot of people think I am a Dalmatian or a "fire dog" because of my spots. The vet says I'm actually part German short-haired pointer and part hound dog, but nobody knows for sure. All I know is...

    I am purposefully unique, just like you!

If you look closely you can see that my spots are actually on my skin, not on my fur like a Dalmatian's spots are.

All of my fur is white except around my ears and face. No other dog has markings exactly like me.

I'm one of a kind!

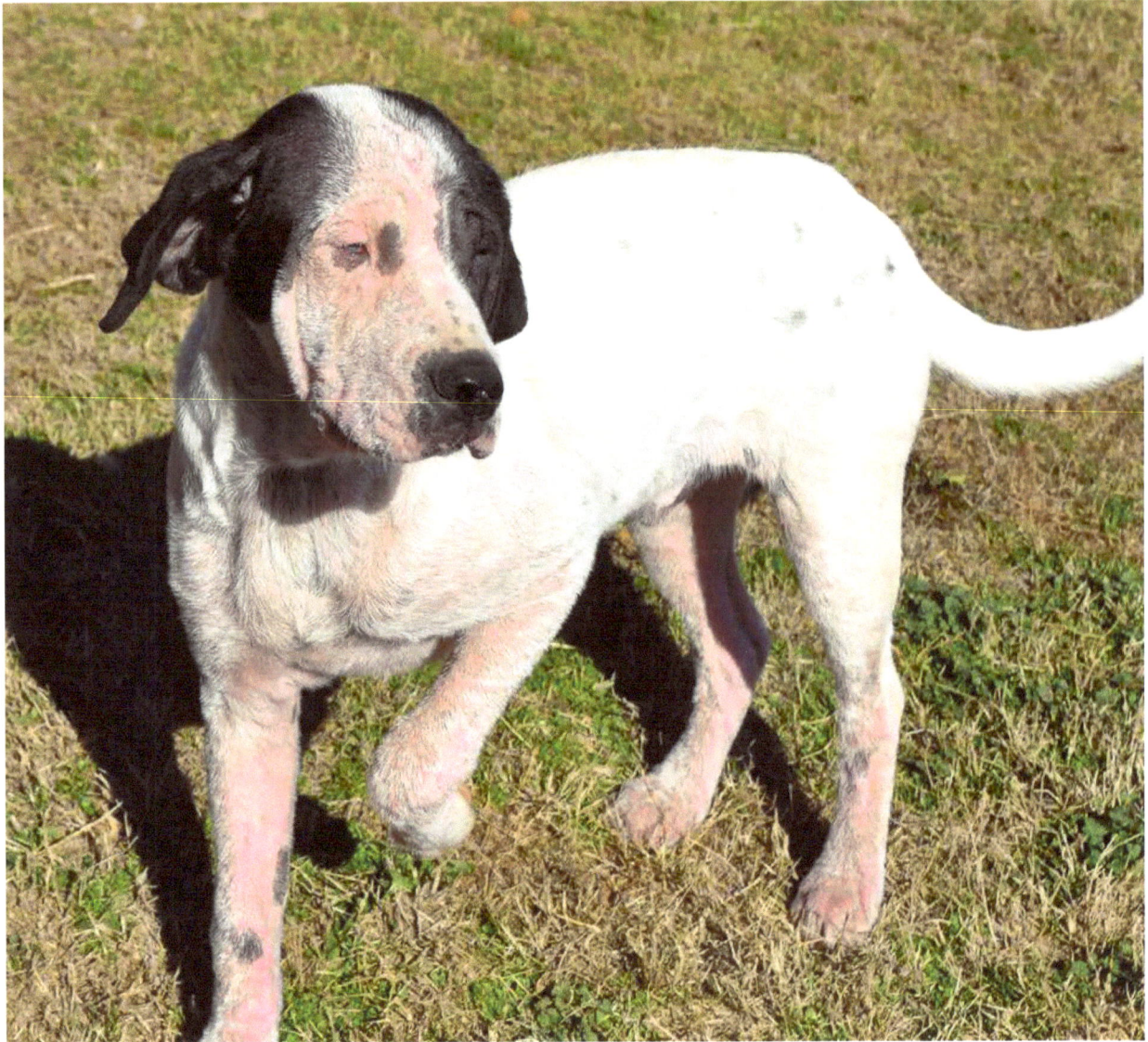

    I wasn't always as handsome as I am now. I was abandoned when I was a young pup so I didn't have anyone to take care of me. I got a skin disease called "mange." It made me very itchy, and I could barely see out of my eyes because they were so swollen.

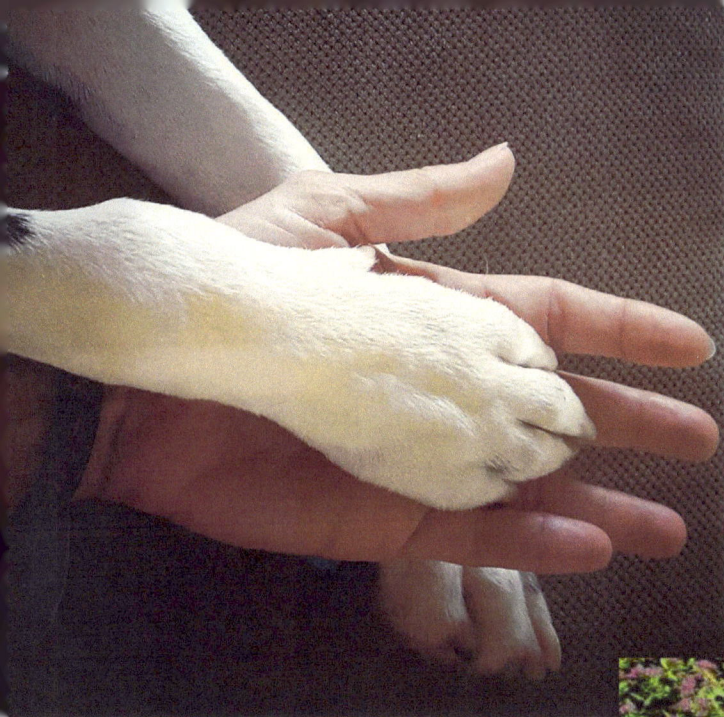

One day, some special people from a group called Rescue Me Georgia found me all alone and in need of help. They were very nice to me and took me to the vet. This was a special ride I call my "freedom ride." I was so grateful that I held my driver's hand for the whole two-hour car trip!

I was given medicine and special baths to make my itchy skin go away. I was so happy that I didn't itch anymore, and I loved playing with all my friends at my new foster home. I had a special way of letting the other dogs know everything was going to be okay. I touched them with my paw and let them know I was their friend.

When my skin disease got better, I had to have an operation on my eyes. If you look closely you can see stitches under my eyes. This is how I got my name, Stitch.

I had a pretty rough start to life, but it never kept me from being happy every single day and loving everyone I met.

One day, the nice people at Rescue Me Georgia brought me to an adoption event with hopes that I would find my forever family. They were right! I was adopted by my "dog-mom," and she loved me the minute she saw me. I was so happy that I was finally going to have a home!

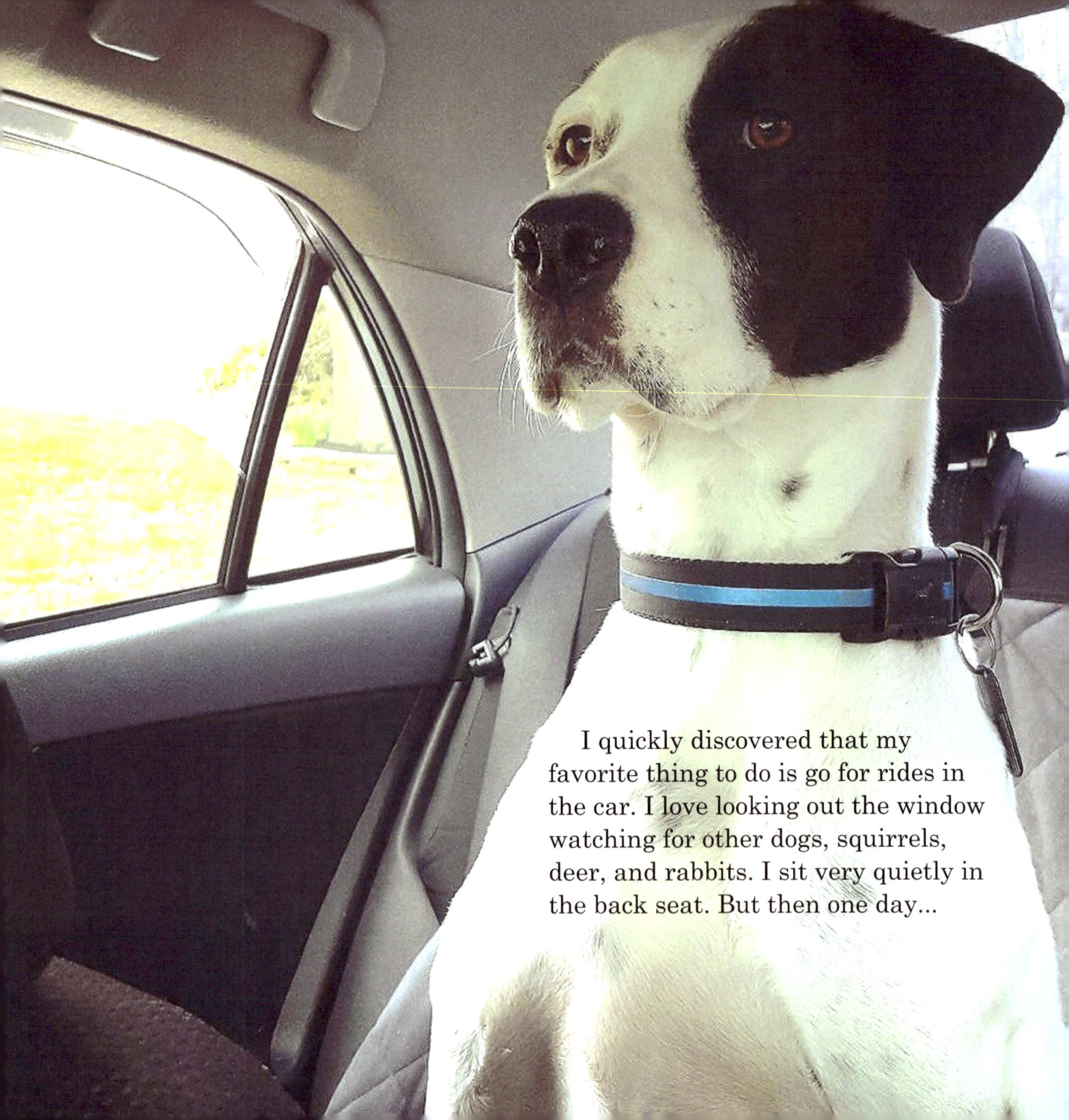

I quickly discovered that my favorite thing to do is go for rides in the car. I love looking out the window watching for other dogs, squirrels, deer, and rabbits. I sit very quietly in the back seat. But then one day...

I saw something out the window that really caught my attention—I think it was a deer! I got so excited and so close to the window that I fell out of the car and broke my leg. My dog-mom quickly stopped the car, picked me up off the side of the road, and sped right to the vet. It was scary, but I knew the people at the animal hospital were taking very good care of me. I had x-rays and an operation to try to fix my leg.

Can you spot my broken bone in the x-ray?

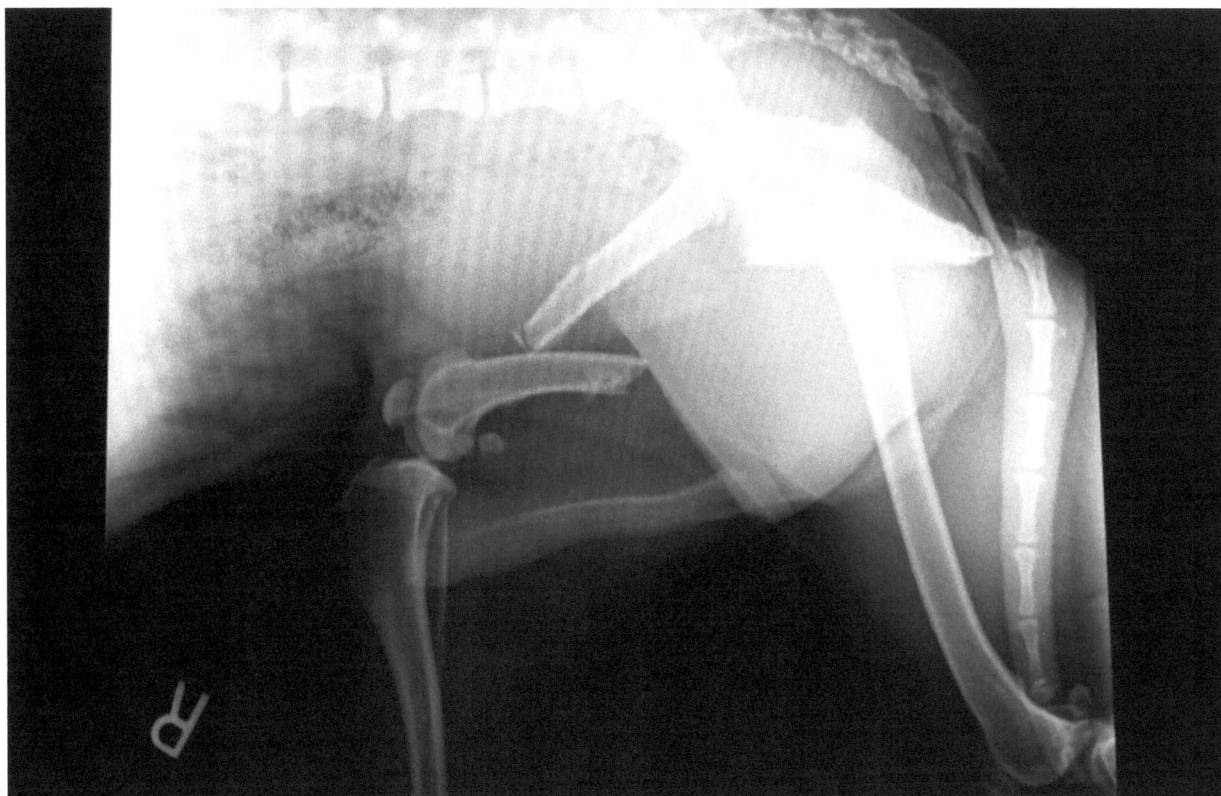

Even though the doctors did their best to fix my broken bone, my leg had to be amputated so it wouldn't hurt me anymore. That is why I only have three legs. It didn't take me long to adapt to my new situation. In fact, I was hopping around the very next day!

Here I am a few weeks after my operation. And now, I don't even notice that my leg is no longer there. I still walk and run with my dog-mom every day. I actually hop instead of walk, but I hop pretty quickly. When I run, I run like the wind—so fast that you would never know I only have three legs!

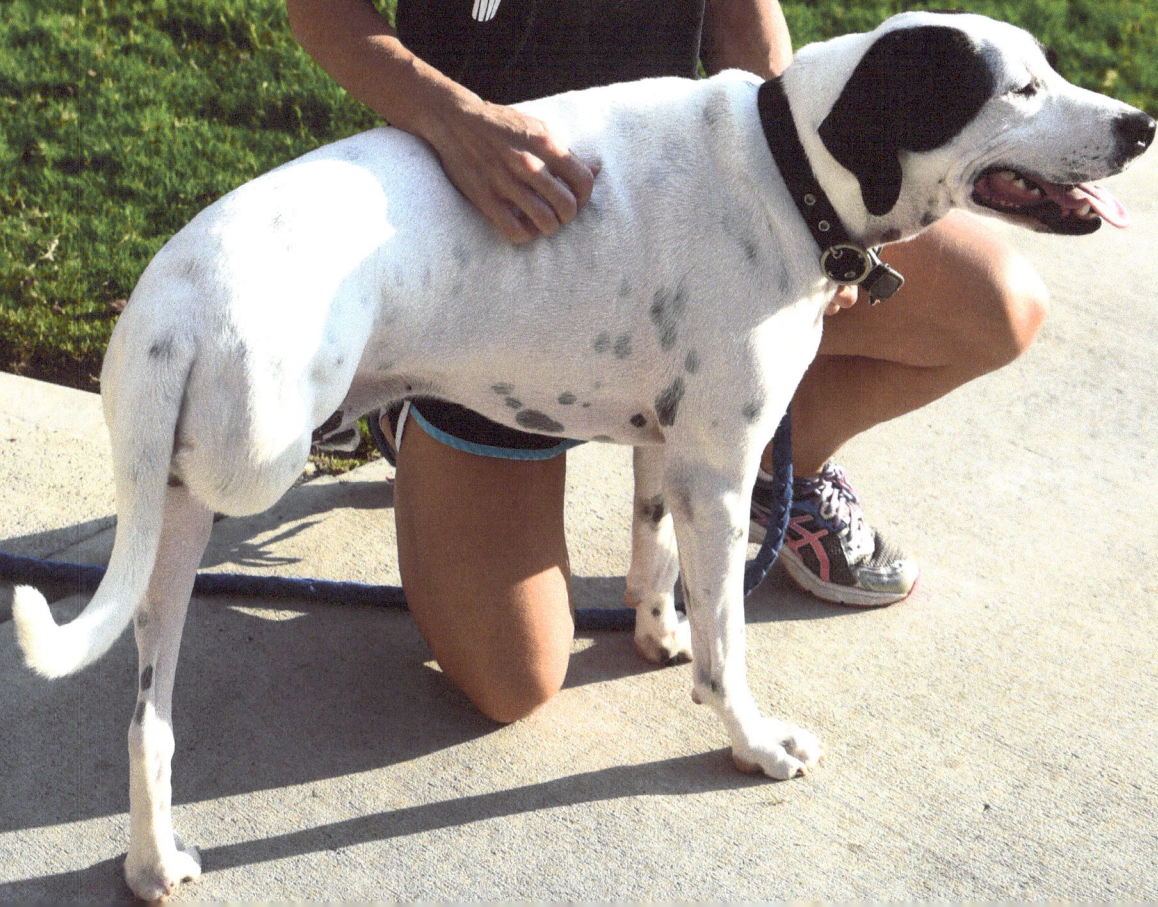

Some people feel sad for me when they notice I only have three legs. I wish they wouldn't. I can still do anything a four-legged dog can do. The trick was to never give up.

Here I am with
some of the things
that make me
very happy:

Watermelon!
Naps!
My toys!

My dog-mom realized I have a very patient and loving personality especially around kids. She thought we should share my gift with others, so I began training to become a therapy dog.

What is a therapy dog?

A therapy dog is a special dog trained to provide love and comfort to people who may be sad, hurt, or in need of a friend. Therapy dogs must be friendly and brave, have good manners, and be good listeners. I am all of these things! When I am working, I wear a red vest, which is my uniform. My vest helps people know who I am and what my job is.

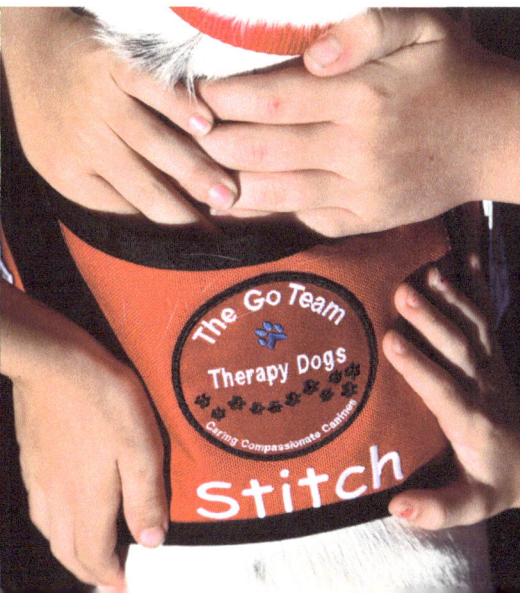

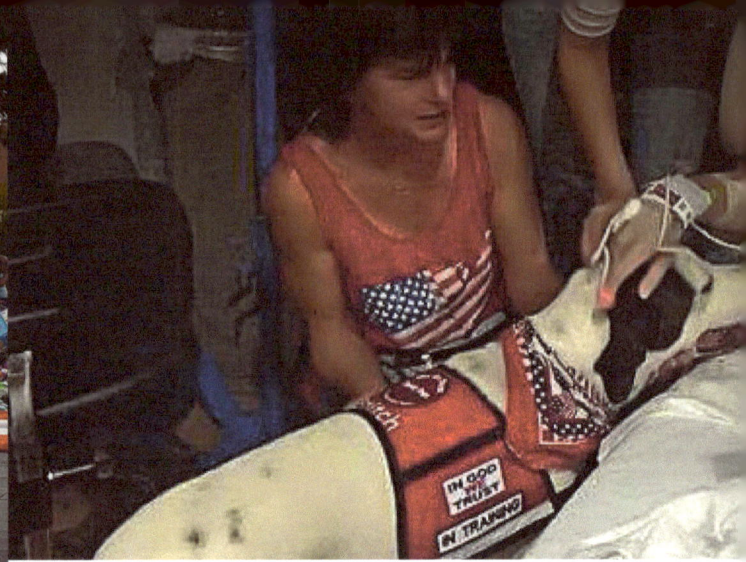

One of my first jobs as a therapy dog was to go to Florida after a lot of people were hurt. My job was just to let people talk to me or hug me. Sometimes, that's all it takes to make someone feel better. I also was asked to go to the hospital and visit people who had been injured. Boy were they surprised to see a dog in the hospital! I made everyone smile that day.

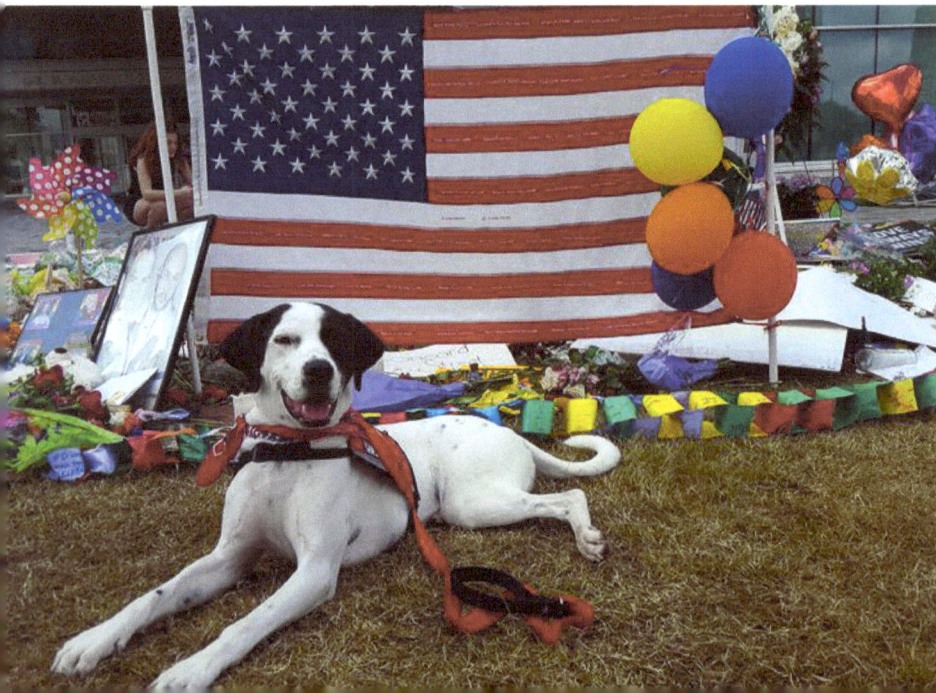

"No act of kindness, no matter how small, is ever wasted."

Aesop

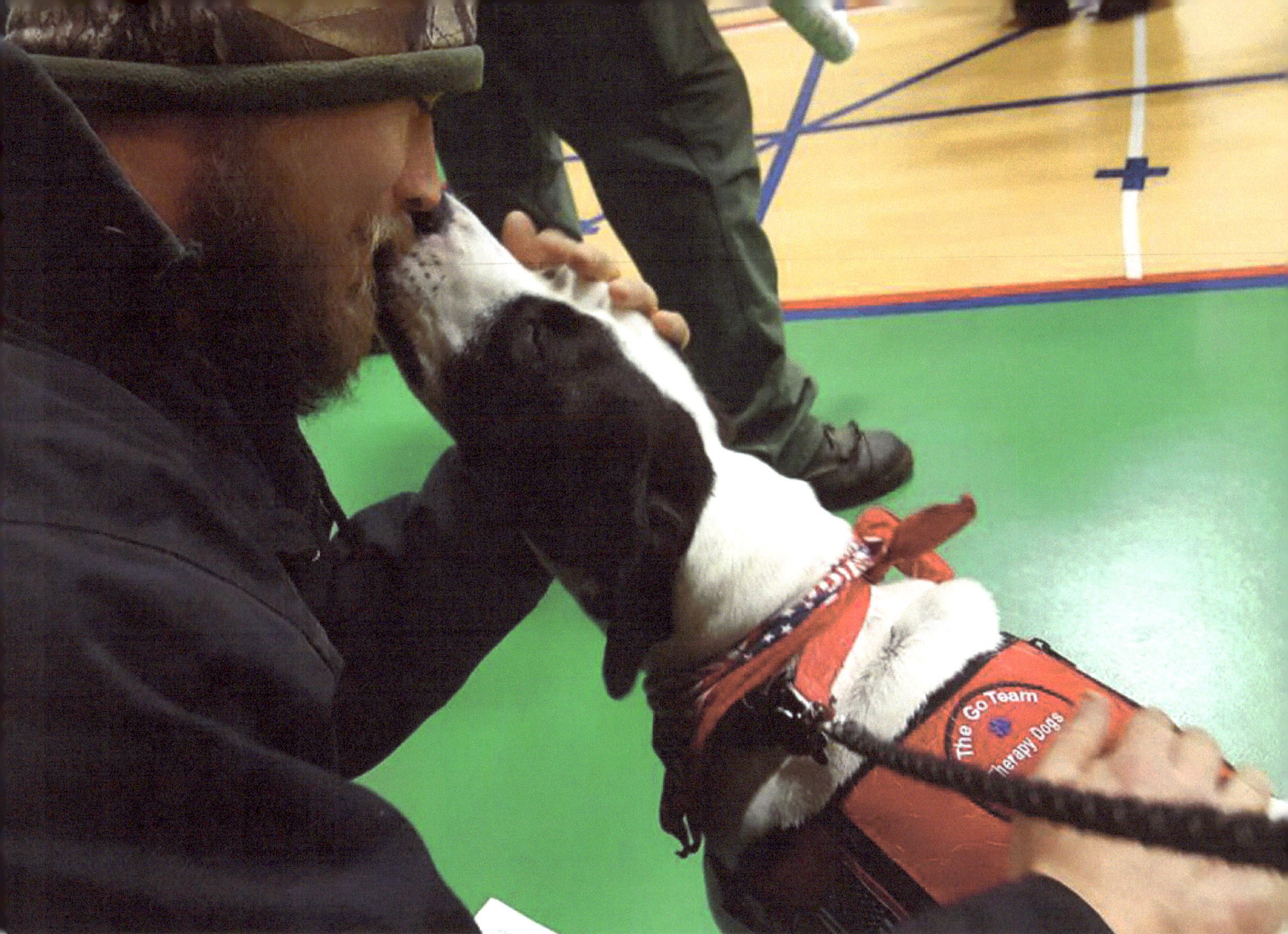

Here I am at a different event—giving encouragement and kisses to a fireman. He was working very hard fighting wildfires that burned for weeks in the north Georgia mountains. Firefighters came from all over the country to help put out the flames. They were tired, hungry, and missing their families. My team and I visited them every morning to let them know how much they were appreciated.

I don't always work, though. Most days I am just a regular ol' silly dog sitting on my front porch watching the world go by.

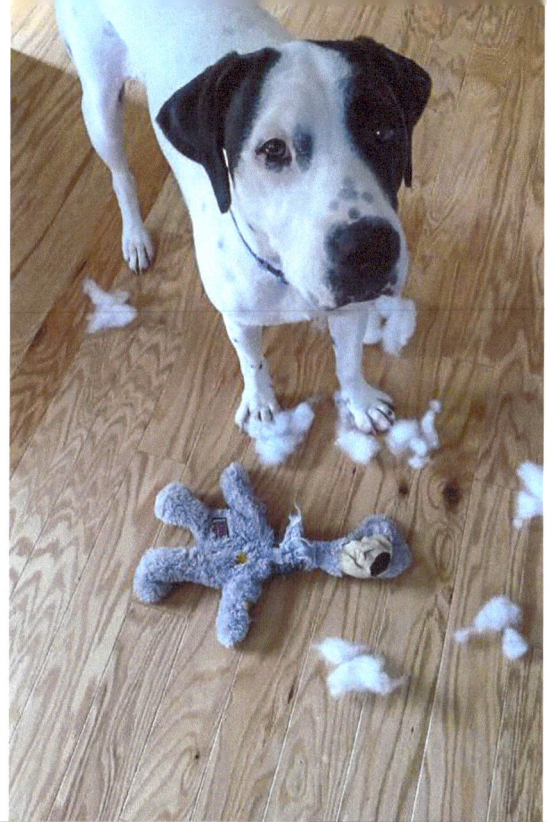

Or just doing what dogs do...

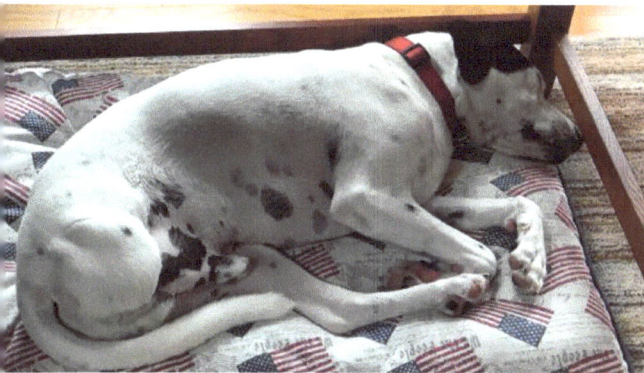

Sometimes I pretend I'm not a dog, but that I'm a pirate sailing the seven seas—or a superhero like Batman chasing villains and helping people!

This is a friend from my neighborhood. She comes to talk to me almost every day. I don't understand everything she says to me because I'm a dog, but her voice is always soft and kind. I just sit quietly and listen and let her hug me until it's time for her to go home. Before she leaves, she always says, "You're a good boy, Stitch. I love you."

"Love is your greatest superpower."
Unknown

I don't know what lies ahead for me, but I do know I will be ready and I will do my best to make a difference.

"Be the change you want to see happen."
Arleen Lorrance

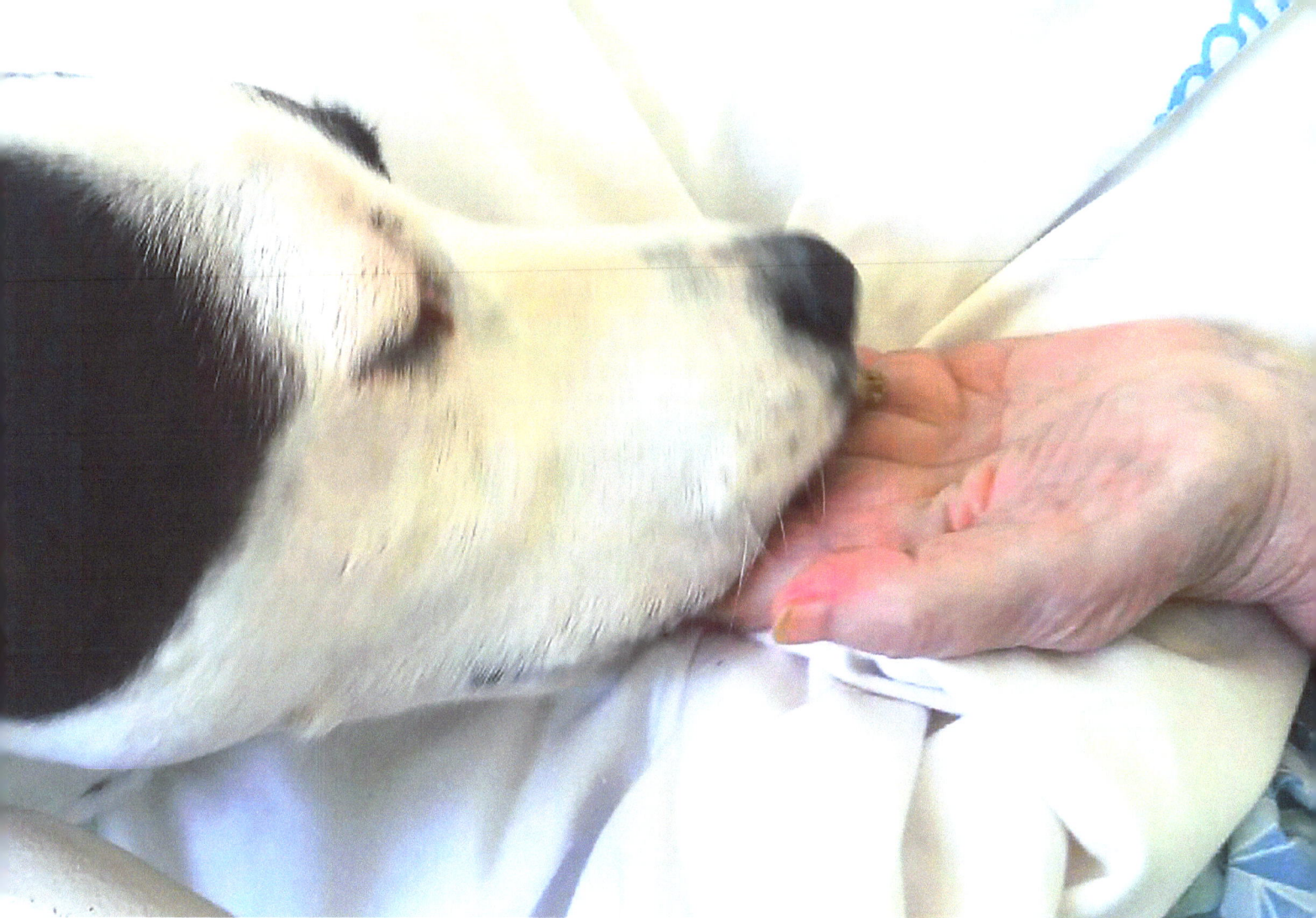

If you believe in the good work I am doing, please visit RMGeorgia.org to learn more about the group that rescued me and helped me find my forever family and purpose.

And I hope to meet you some day!

"No matter what happens in life, be good to people."
Colleen Ritzer

ACKNOWLEDGMENTS

I would like to first thank the many selfless volunteers at Rescue Me Georgia and every other person out there who works tirelessly to rescue animals that have been abandoned, neglected, or abused. It takes a huge heart to sacrifice a part of yours to help those who cannot help themselves. I thank you from the bottom of my heart for loving Stitch first and giving him his second chance.

I also thank the brave kids that Stitch and I have met through Camp No Limits (NoLimitsFoundation.org). You, like Stitch, make this world a brighter place by overcoming your adversity with smiles, strength, and contagious courage.

Thank you, Kathy Orzech, for your unwavering support and guidance every step of the way.

Thank you to Andrew Chapman and Social Motion Publishing for believing in *Stitch's Story* and being the platform to share his story to kids of all ages. Your patience and mission is a testament to the old adage that no act of kindness is ever wasted. You are making a lasting difference.

Lastly, thank you for buying a copy of *Stitch's Story* and sharing it with others. May you find a part of his story within your own story and know you are brave, you are strong, and you have a special purpose. Go out and make your mark on the world. Smile and be kind—the world needs more of that.

ABOUT THE AUTHOR & PHOTOGRAPHER

For almost two decades as a police officer in Massachusetts, Laura Fogarty performed regular assigned duties as well as crime scene investigations, tactical photography, and training. It was in doing so that she was introduced to the value of photography to tell a story.

When she retired from law enforcement, Fogarty moved to Georgia where she started her own photography business. Laura Fogarty Tactical Photography is dedicated to supporting the relentless pursuit of justice throughout the country. (LauraFogartyPhotography.com)

In addition to her photography, Fogarty continues to use her forensic knowledge to assist agencies in locations around the globe. She is the very proud mother of a U.S. Army soldier and volunteers her time in support of Stitch's work as a therapy dog.

Fogarty is a firm believer in that, by helping others, we help ourselves and our ultimate goal here on earth is to leave it better than we found it.

"Then I heard the voice of the Lord say,
Whom shall I send? Who will go for us?"
And I said, "Here I am. Send me."
Isaiah 6:8

ABOUT RESCUE ME GEORGIA

Two women came together in 2012 with the same passion and dedication—to help the forgotten dogs of Jasper County, about 50 miles southeast of Atlanta.

Shelia Fielding and Marybeth Rathbun decided to concentrate their efforts on a small rural animal control in Monticello, Georgia, and created Rescue Me Georgia, an all-volunteer 501(c)3 nonprofit licensed rescue organization. Because most of their foster homes are around Atlanta, RMG volunteers spend a lot of time transporting animals between the two areas, sometimes running 24/7. But despite the challenges, RMG has grown year after year and saved the lives of more than 5,000 dogs.

For more information, please check out the organization's website at RMGdogs.org.

www.ingramcontent.com/pod-product-compliance
Lightning Source LLC
Chambersburg PA
CBHW041222040426

42443CB00002B/57